A Day at School

Dona Herweck Rice

Get Ready

wake up

eat breakfast

brush teeth

get dressed

pack bag

Go to School

walk

climb stairs

ride a bike

ride a bus

ride in a car

Greetings

say hello

shake hands

wave

smile

high five

People at School

student

teacher

principal

custodian

class

School Supplies

books

pencils

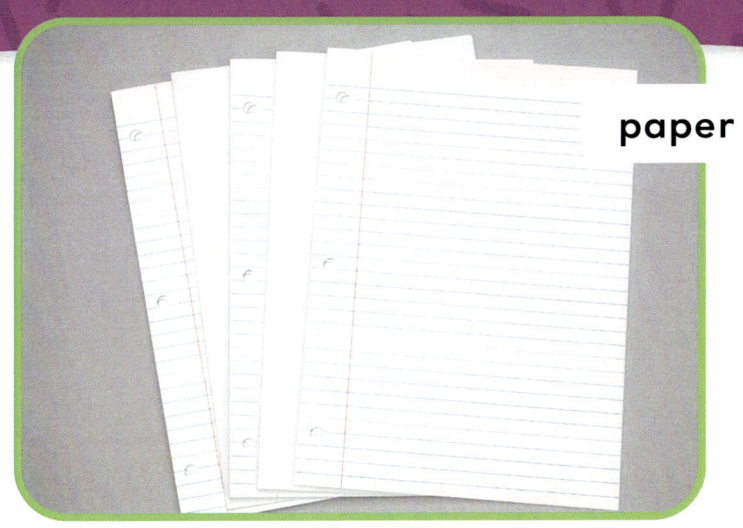

paper

markers

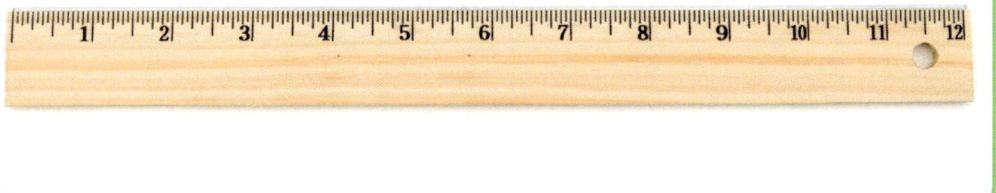

ruler

Recess

play

talk

jump

run

be with friends

School Rules

line up

listen

raise your hand

walk, don't run

be kind

How We Learn

teacher

computer

partners

small group

class

Lunchtime

eat

drink

sit

clean up

use manners

Subjects

reading

writing

math

science

social studies

Go Home

put away

pack bag

say goodbye

leave

do homework

Consultants
Jessica Lang, M.A. Ed.
Elementary Teacher, Los Angeles

Publishing Credits
Rachelle Cracchiolo, M.S.Ed., *Publisher*
Emily R. Smith, M.A.Ed., *SVP of Content Development*
Véronique Bos, *VP of Creative*
Fabiola Sepulveda, *Art Director*

Image Credits: all images from iStock, Shutterstock, or in the public domain

Library of Congress Control Number available upon request.

5482 Argosy Avenue
Huntington Beach, CA 92649
www.tcmpub.com
ISBN 979-8-3309-0482-2
© 2025 Teacher Created Materials, Inc.